WHAT MAKES AN ACTOR?

A DIRECTOR'S VIEW OF ACTING

Dorothy Marie Robinson

ISBN 978-0-615-35175-9

FIRST EDITION April 2010

Blue Ball PUBLISHING

Find us on facebook.com

Printed in the United States of America

This book is dedicated to Marie E. O'Brien
who introduced me to theatre in high school.

It's also for Mary K. Hurt and Jay Silverman.

WHAT MAKES AN ACTOR?

"How do you act?"a respected colleague asked me.

Because the question was sincere, I made an attempt to answer it in a brief and honest way. The next day I smiled, remembering how I blathered on about finding clues in the script, various rehearsal techniques, and a way to go forward with trust. I also began contemplating a more comprehensive response.

A week later another person asked if I could advise someone with acting experience on how to direct a play. Two days later, a friend of many years called and said she had a dream that I wrote a book with the title What Makes An Actor? A Director's View of Acting. Hmmmmmm.

I had no interest in writing a full-length dissertation, but I decided to put together a practical, concise, easy-to-read handbook. This is the result. It contains my collected thoughts and suggestions relative to the question, as well as a few "secrets." By secret I mean a personal piece of useful information or advice.

Drawing on over fifty-years of experience, the first section of the book is based on my work as an actor and teacher; the second section takes a look at acting through the eyes of a director.

My intention was to write for both the student and the experienced actor—something to refer to if feeling stuck or if wondering what you might be forgetting in your work. It should open some doors and give you encouragement to go deeper into an area of particular interest. There's a list of books for further reading on pages 68-69.

Let me say, too, that this guide primarily addresses the stage actor but much of it crosses over to other media. For purposes of communication I use examples from movies and television as well as live theatre.

The first part of this handbook contains the down-and-dirty, cut-to-the-chase, must-have fundamentals for the actor in ten chapters.

Number 10.

I want to start with the last chapter first. You could call it a dramatic device, but your attention is already on what you just read, and rehearsal is always first, last, and in-between. Everyone knows that "Practice!" is the answer to "How do you get to Carnegie Hall?" Anyone learning an instrument, a song, or dance, or a poem, or preparing a manuscript or speech, has heard the same prompting as the actor, which is—

ONE MORE TIME

Rehearsal doesn't just mean repetition. Yes, it means doing it over and over, but each time you incorporate more nuance, establish a flow, build confidence, and add depth of character. Practice means to refine and polish and then do it again, *as if for the first time.*

Practice also means to get experience by doing—performing as much as possible in front of an audience or camera—getting feedback from trusted sources—an ongoing, life-long venture.

Obviously you are interested in acting or you wouldn't be reading this, but do you know why? Is it really an art? When you see how convincingly people can lie about a clandestine affair or to get out of a traffic ticket, you might say, "Anyone can be an actor, what's the big deal?" The truth is that almost anyone *can* do it, at least once, if the stakes are high enough. But acting is not telling lies for five minutes.

What is it then?

Acting is best known and valued as a method for relating story. Throughout the world, stories are shared as a means of entertainment, education, enlightenment, to instill moral values, and preserve culture.

The **art** of acting is being able to understand a script, create a three-dimensional character, make the fictional stakes real and urgent, and repeat your same performance *time after time* for a paying audience—an audience that is hungry for truth, and beauty, and inspiration, and laughter, and insight into the human condition.

And why would you want to act for a career? If your answer to this question is "I just want to be famous," I wish you good luck. I personally like the response expressed in a line from *The Rainmaker* by Richard Nash. The character of Lizzie says, "I get so tired of me. Just once, I'd like to get outside of me and be somebody else."

Acting as an art form is a noble profession and deserves respect. If you ever doubt that, ponder or meditate on this: **Through the alchemy of acting, ideas and mere words on a piece of paper are transformed—brought to *life*.** Wow! What a profound human ability.

If you are driven to live a creative life no matter the difficulty, you have every right to go for it. Be aware, however, that your family may not understand or support you in this decision, unless they are artists, too.

Number 9.

IT'S ALIVE

Unless I'm stuck with a one-dimensional character in a so-so script, a character does not creep up on me. I either have it or I don't. Yes, layers will be added incrementally during rehearsal and with research, but the "this is it" impulse arrives fully formed. My task is to find or recognize "it."

Sometimes this kernal comes in discovering a gesture, the perfect shoes, a vocal quality, a walk, an inner sense of being, or danger, or ambition, or—best of all—**a secret**. You know it when you find it. Of course if you don't find or recognize "it," you have to make the whole thing up which is harder and rarely as satisfying! A painting, a piece of music, a photograph can help. As I write this, Golden Globe winner Paul Giamatti has just said his wig was the catalyst to playing John Adams. Meryl Streep said she used knitting offstage to inform the prayerful diligence of her nun in *Doubt*.

To be honest, the catalyst usually comes to me the first time I read the script. A line my character says or that someone else says about my character pops out and has a resonance within my personal tuning fork. From some other realm of deep knowing, there it is . . . my connection. It is an element of truth against which all other choices can be measured.

Secret. When I find this special line, it is often two-thirds of the way into the play. By the time I reach performance level, just saying the line to myself can propel me into character. It is a touchstone I go to before my first entrance.

By the way, never share your character prompt or secret with anyone or it will dry up for you. Forget the many theories about why this happens—just know that it does.

Many ideas come from asking the question "What If ;" and the following anecdote will explain something valuable called "As If ."

During the time she dominated television in the *I Love Lucy* show, I had the privilege of sitting down with the comedic genius, Lucille Ball. I retain three important things from that informal gathering:

> **One.** Before she was famous, her discovery of a book called *The Art of Selfishness* gave her some much-needed self-esteem.
>
> **Two.** After achieving success, she contacted many of the actors she had known "before," inviting them to join her in California and work on the show. Not one of them took her up on the offer! There were many "good reasons," but not one jumped at the opportunity. She came to the conclusion that many actors are content to hang around the periphery of the profession. [Or, as I once read, *"He prefers living the life of the artist to making art."*]
>
> **Three.** She had the ability to totally believe what she was doing, as she did it. If the script said a piece of toast pops into the air, it never occurred to her that it was actually a prop piece of wood, it was toast to her.

This third thing is the magical and essential quality that is referred to as behaving "As If." **The ability to pretend . . . to play . . . is what brings your efforts to life.**

Number 8.

NERVES (Oh My God!)

Unless you're a narcissist or total egoist you will experience stage fright. It's natural to want to do well. And the bottom line is, **you have to be willing to make a fool of yourself**.

The best defense is to be well rehearsed and *know that the audience wants you to do well*. They will send you positive energy once you get out there. The initial waiting and first step onto the stage are hardest, and then the trick is to stay focused. Stay anchored in the moment; talk and listen.

The best teacher I ever had said to consider many different choices during rehearsal; that way, one of them will always be there for you.

Secret. Before you step onstage, really look at something on your person closely: a watch, a ring, the back of your hand, a fingernail. Notice everything about it as if you had to describe or draw it perfectly. What are the details that make it unique? Zero in. When you hear your cue, step out on stage. Having concentrated on something else, you are ready to give your full attention to the play.

A favorite story of mine came from a dear actor named Gwyllum Evans:

> Mitzi was a Ziegfield Follies showgirl who suffered from stage fright and was scared of heights.
>
> The girls made their initial entrance down a long, steep set of stairs in high heels, and Mitzi had never once done it right. She always broke step or looked down, but everyone knew she needed the job and

covered for her. On opening night, however, Mitzi sailed beautifully down and everyone rushed up to her after the number. "It was perfect," they said, "we're so proud of you. How did you do it?"

"Well," said Mitzi, "I just stood at the top of those stairs, looked out at the audience and said to myself, 'God is Love, fuck it all,' and down I went."

And this mind-set worked for her every time.

Can you step into the abyss of not knowing? It is a paradox. You have to go forward on trust and not dwell on the fact that at any moment something unexpected can happen. You need the courage to go into the burning building, but you must also have the right training and gear.

What makes acting thrilling for both the actor and audience is that element of danger. Notice I do not say real danger but the possibility of danger.

Number 7.

PROTOCOL

Arrive at least five minutes early to rehearsal and carry a pencil.

Write down your blocking. Use a pencil because some of it will change.

Put your name on your script. Always know where it is.

If you are late, you are inconsiderate of others and will probably feel shunned all day. You must get permission to arrive late—and it is not given easily. If you are not at rehearsal, you make it hard on everyone. "The show must go on" is still a law of the theatre as far as I know.

BE QUIET when you are offstage. Others are working.

On show days, sign in yourself no later than half-hour before curtain.

Respect the fact that many actors don't want to be interrupted in the dressing room or backstage. They use this time for preparation.

Figure out what you need and want, and find a nice way to let company members know whether or not you want them to talk to you. It's enough to quietly say, "I don't talk backstage," or "Not right now, please."

During rehearsal or inside the theater environs, it's considered bad luck to whistle or say *Macbeth*. It is referred to as "the Scottish play."

NEVER tell another actor what to do; address them through the director or stage manager if it's essential.

The actress Cleo Holladay has written a wonderful booklet on theatre protocol. An important rule is to say, "thank you" when a stage manager calls "half-hour," "fifteen minutes," "five minutes," and "places."

Always hang up your costumes!

Number 6.

MUSIC / TIMING

I put these two together because good timing is like music—it has a rhythm.

Can you learn it or do you have to be born with it? Everyone I know who **has** good timing says it can't be taught. One thing is sure—we know it when we see it. But the jury is still out on this one, because I've seen lots of people blossom over time. And you do have help, because one of the main tasks of a director is to determine the pacing of a production.

> *Timing is defined as the ability to select the precise moment for doing something for optimum effect. Nowhere is this more necessary than in comedy.*

On his deathbed, Bert Lahr, the cowardly lion in the *Wizard of Oz,* was asked by a friend, "Tell me Bert, how is it, what is dying like?" His famous answer was, "It's not as hard as playing comedy."

Think for a minute about how many different types of comedy are out there. Physical comedy [slapstick] has been around the longest. There's fast-paced, door-slamming farce, and comedy of manners and situation. Mark Twain tells humorous stories. Stand-up comedians use jokes.

In the play *The Sunshine Boys,* by Neil Simon, one of the characters says words with "k" are funnier than other words. "Chicken is funny. Pickle is funny. Cupcake is funny. Tomato is not funny."

The "rule of three" means that a joke often has an uneven rhythm—three, five, or seven—with the last beat [the topper or punch line] being the pay off—the one that gets the biggest laugh.

Victor Borge combined comedic timing and music brilliantly. He would ask, "Is there anyone who would like to hear the famous *Polonaise in A Flat* by Chopin? " After hearing the inevitable calls of "Yes, yes," Borge would respond, "Very well, is there anyone here who can play it?"

Even if you don't want to be a comedian or perform in musicals, take classes in singing and dancing to improve your timing. It may be the best gift you will ever give yourself. And learn to read the language of music if you have the chance—if only to have the joy of being in a chorus.

Number 5.

WHAT DO I DO WITH MY HANDS?

Nothing. You let your arms hang at your side, elbows slightly out, and don't move them unless you shake hands, embrace, or make a needed gesture. Don't twitch, rub, pick, or signal anything the way you've seen it done in the movies. On stage, it draws focus and confuses the audience.

If you are sitting, lay one hand on top of the other and let it stay there. Figure out how you want to position your feet and don't move them.

Once you learn to do nothing, you can begin to incorporate selective movement.

WALKING ■ FALLING ■ SITTING ■ STEPS

You probably already know some of the following basics for actors, but I'm sure you'll find a few surprises.

We walk down the street, we *cross* on stage. In most cases, it's more interesting to put a little arc in your cross, rather than crossing directly to your destination.

It's important to create for yourself a *shorthand* so you can notate your blocking quickly. [Example: XR = cross Right; XL = cross Left; X2Chr = cross to chair; V = sit; Λ = rise; XULC = cross Upstage Left of Center.]

Stage Right is to the actor's right if he's facing the audience. In creating a stage picture the director may say, "move a little toward stage Right or I'd like you Down Right Center."

Stage Positions.

UR	URC	UC	ULC	UL	[UPSTAGE]
R	RC	**C**	LC	**L**	[CENTER STAGE]
DR	DRC	DC	DLC	DL	[DOWNSTAGE]

Upstage is away from the audience or camera. A stage used to be built on a slope (raked) so the audience could see better. To walk away from the audience was to literally walk up the stage.

If you are working in the round, stage positions are indicated as clock times (i.e., Jack is at 4 o'clock, Tom at 8 o'clock). Center stage is always Center stage.

Body Positions. In addition to your stage position, your body position also has a designation. A director will often be very specific about this if there are more than four actors onstage.

Full Front (FF) means you are fully facing the audience and Full Back (FB) means you are turned away from the audience facing Upstage. Facing Right or facing Left is obvious, but to complicate it, this is also called Profile, or if you are talking with another actor, the director may say, "share the scene" (face each other).

Standing One-Quarter Right or One-Quarter Left, however, is the most used body position. It's not FF or Profile but in-between.

Standing Three-Quarters Right or Three-Quarters Left is in between Profile and FB.

There is also something called "countering" that's very important. It has to do with the law of cause and effect. If someone else moves on stage, you will need to make a slight adjustment to your body or stage position—with time, it will become intuitive. [Example: If someone is to cross in front of you, you must anticipate it, and step back a little as they approach.]

Falling. Generally you work backwards on this one. Where does the director want you to end up? Then you slowly work out how to land there. The best way to fall is on your side, rolling onto your thigh and butt—where there is the most padding—and then on down, being careful not to bang your head. There should be a special rehearsal to work out the details but give it some thought on your own.

Practice on a mat and do it in slow motion until you are comfortable increasing the speed. *It's up to you to make sure you do not get hurt*. Remember, you can refuse to do something dangerous to your well-being.

Sitting. Sit without looking at the seat—no more than a quick glance—have it in your peripheral vision. Approach the seat and turn your back when you get directly in front of it, feel the front of the bench or chair with the back of your leg, and then sit. Unless it's a character choice, don't flop or slouch in the chair; maintain your balance so you can rise smoothly. Practice doing this a couple of times and you'll become quite good at it.

Be aware of your leg position while sitting; don't shift around unless you are talking. If you are wearing a skirt, check to see what you might be exposing.

Steps. Just like sitting, don't keep looking down once you take the first step. Coming down, slide the back of your heel down the step riser as a guide. All the steps are the same size and height, so if you start out well, you're okay. If the tread is too short for your foot, you may have to place your foot a little sideways as you go down or up. Remember, the stage lights can be blinding, so always try the steps before you need to use them, and figure it out.

Not Tripping. If you will be wearing a long skirt, or have a cape, or sword, or heels, or hat, or even a coat, you need to rehearse with some temporary garment that offers the same challenges. Once the scene is blocked, you need to work in clothing similar to your costume. Rehearsing in jeans, tennis shoes, and a tee shirt will not serve you well in a period piece. Pros know that to get their show shoes early—and rehearse in them—is a big advantage.

THE KISS AND THE SLAP

Both must be choreographed, most especially any physical fighting. It must be done over and over in slow motion until there is certain knowledge of safety. Stage combat is actually fun because you barely touch one another; it's acting and illusion. The reaction is what sells the slap or punch. As a director, I fire any actor who is reckless with safety. There is no excuse for someone being hurt.

The opposite is true of the kiss. You must touch. Your upper thighs must come together and you must plan where your feet go—like a close dance. If you are toe to toe, it looks like a pup tent. There is an unspoken pact between actors; when playing love scenes, *you are doing a job.* No matter how passionate the physical connection, it only exists while rehearsing or performing.

The first few times the scene is often "marked" or done technically. At some point one of the actors or the director will say something like, "let's go for it today" which is permission to play the scene fully and up to speed.

There is a line you do not cross. *You do not put your tongue in your partner's mouth* unless it is discussed first. And I don't know how or when this open-mouth devouring kind of kiss got started but it's rarely necessary. I guess it's supposed to say "uncontrolled passion." It hardly reads as love, tenderness, or respect. Of course your mouth should be slightly open, and then I beg you to linger and not do a bunch of those gobble-like kisses. I feel so disappointed when supposed lovers give each other a quick kiss and a pat.

You're right; it's not easy. That's why you rehearse.

Number 4.

■ BUILDS AND FOCUS

What is a build? When I tell a story or want to make a point, I *build* to a punch line. To begin with, I set up the scene and characters clearly, somewhat slowly, so there's no confusion. I then involve the listener by changing the pace and intensity of what I'm saying, perhaps bringing in a surprise or diversion for interest, but always heading toward the punch line. And then there's a reaction and release—and another build starts. A build can last a page or most of an act. The longer it lasts, the more skill it takes.

The actor must create a kind of tension toward a chosen climax. This keeps the audience engaged. The easiest example is to consider an argument, which gradually accelerates by fits and starts to what appears to be an out-of-control slap. Not only do the words come out faster and louder, but the character increasingly "has more at stake" until someone wins or loses—by force, by leaving, by giving up . . . whatever is written.

These builds and releases create the success or failure of a piece of theatre. They are the technical scaffolding on which everything else is hinged. If an actor changes what he or she is doing and draws focus away from the person or build that was rehearsed, the point is lost. Over time, you develop a sense of when to take focus and give focus in order to propel the story of the play along. The director helps with this.

> *An example of taking focus when you shouldn't is moving or walking on another actor's important line. Unless you are directed otherwise, it's better to move when you are speaking.*

Learning to express the "pregnant pause" is a powerful tool, but must not be overused.

Secret. Punctuation is used for reader clarity. A comma or period in the script does not necessarily indicate the best place to pause or take a breath in dialogue.

Number 3.

THE NITTY-GRITTY

SENSE MEMORY

Let's start with "The Method." The Russian actor and director Constantin Stanislavsky noticed that if one got quiet and contacted the memory of a place, or event, or emotion, one could look around and explore it. You can do this . . . take a deep breath . . . go to your favorite place and relax. Breathe. Relax. Remember.

Stanislavsky had the idea that through the use of this human ability, his acting ensemble might communicate with an audience in a more authentic way. They created exercises designed to remember, explore, engage the senses, deconstruct and reconstruct feelings and images. They sought to recreate the reality of a past experience in present time. He wrote several books about this exploration.

Some of Stanislavsky's students, most notably Richard Boleslavsky and Maria Ouspenskaya, and then Stella Adler, Lee Strasberg, and Sanford Meisner developed this concept in America.

We were all thrilled with the nuance, the sensuality, and the soulfulness of this revolutionary approach. Director Elia Kazan, playwright Tennessee Williams, and actor Marlon Brando are well-known personalities who fostered this kind of work along with many, *many* others. Audience members laughed and cried and were in pain right along with the performers. It felt real—as if it were actually happening in that place and time.

However thrilling it might be, there is a possible down side to this innovative process. Some actors get so absorbed in their role that it seems as if they are channeling another entity. Even though they often brag about this ability, I feel the necessity to mention the need for some caution. Why? Because it may be harmful—and nobody wants to act with someone who is out-of-their-body, out-of-control, or overly-self-involved.

Once, in a rehearsal of *Threepenny Opera,* I had an actor slap me so hard I saw stars and nearly fell down some steps. I stopped the rehearsal. This actor protested that he was sure his character beat his wife; that he wasn't sure where the need to whack me came from; he just felt it come over him. "That may be so," I said to him in front of the director, "but don't ever hit me again unless it's rehearsed."

Uta Hagen, my mentor and teacher, cautioned that no matter how caught up you might be in your role, it is essential to be present enough to know if something is about to fall on your head. I believe she felt there were many abuses and misunderstandings about "The Method." In class I heard her say more than once, "What you are doing is not acting; this is something that needs to be dealt with in therapy."

This is a good time to mention that Hagen wrote what to me is the definitive in-depth training book, *A Challenge for the Actor.* She includes a wonderful history of acting in the chapter titled "An Actor's World."

It does fascinate me that what is referred to as "The Method" came along at exactly the right time to be incorporated into movies and television. It's perfect for film. The camera loves to move in and play with an actor's tear, or quivering lip, capture a whisper, or eyes that reflect complex inner thought.

This technique does not always lend itself to live theatre, however. It can be difficult for the audience to see or hear unless they are sitting quite close. The stage actor has to create and communicate what I would call a believable semblance of reality, and find the best way to project it through gesture, tone of voice and body position relative to the audience and other performers. And what about farce and musicals? Do they really lend themselves to "Method" acting? Today's actor has to be very flexible.

Whatever your method of getting in touch with honest feelings, it is something you will need to explore. **As an actor you must have access to your emotions and be able to express them.**

IMAGINATION

As actors, we draw on our own personal history in various ways to make something real. Memories and intuition are often all that's needed, but nothing is as fertile to draw from as the imagination. When you are called upon to act something that you have not literally experienced in real life, you have to come up with a substitute and apply it.

> Example: What if you're supposed to murder someone? You might say, "I've never had that impulse." But haven't you at one time or another hated a fly or mosquito so much for pestering you, you'd stalk it and do anything to kill it?

Substitutions are also good to use for props and relationships with other characters. Ask yourself, "What valuable and precious book or family heirloom do I own that might inform the way I handle a certain prop? Which relative or friend do I feel the same about as the character in this play?" And remember the importance of "When is this all taking place?" Be specific as to year, season, month, day, hour.

> *The more your imagination is charged by a substitute, the more ripe your performance.*

Don't forget to ask, "Where am I?" It's helpful to seek out a room or space similar to the one called for in the play. Walk around in it and use your imagination. What would you be doing in this space outside of the scene you are to play? Are you comfortable? What do you like about it? Imagine how you would function in it on a daily basis. Further, have you made real to yourself the country, and city, and neighborhood where your character lives?

Museums, historical homes, paintings, movies, and travel are splendid for jogging the imagination. It doesn't matter if it's exact—it matters if it is a good substitution. Years ago, I was struggling to make real the bedroom in *Othello* and found a room at the Metropolitan Museum of Art that seemed a possibility. I couldn't do this now, but when no one was looking, I slipped under the cord and stood inside the space, and imagination did the rest.

Many actors who are serious about their work, like to write an imagined biography of their character's life.

Among my papers, I came across a post-it note with six items on it: ART, EDUCATION, RELIGION, PATRIARCHAL VALUES, PARENTING, DRUGS. Consider the effect of each of them on your character. [To what degree has your own life been influenced by these six things?]

MEMORIZATION ■ OBJECTIVES ■ OBSTACLES

How do you learn all those lines?

Along with that often heard question is another saying that applies, "Use it or lose it." The exercise of committing something to memory is somewhat like building up a muscle. It also takes an ability to concentrate. For me, concentration requires carving out an uninterrupted span of time in a space without noise. If the script is well written and has a logical flow, the job is easier.

Before the push to memorize, I think it's better to break down the script. What is the purpose of this play? Why was it written? What does the playwright want the audience to go away with? How does my character fit into the overall picture? Figure out that A leads to B, which leads to C, and then D, and finally E. These are the broad strokes of painting the background of your character canvas and are pretty easy to remember. [NOTE: If it turns out the director has a totally different take on the script, your work is not in vain. It will just require an adjustment, and that adjustment provides a further way to get familiar with the script.]

Next, you figure out or create the OBJECTIVES. There is the main/overall objective (sometimes called the "arc" or spine) and then an objective of a particular act or scene.

Objectives within a scene are referred to as "beats" or actions. There are many small plays within every play—indeed within every scene—sometimes on each page of the script. ***When a character is on stage, he or she wants something***. The "beat" is how that plays out. This "want" will either succeed or fail and thus a new "beat" will begin.

> *"Want" implies lack of something desired, or craved, or longed for. Need. Wishes.*

You gradually give a title to all these little plays within the scene and can create what I call an **action score**. Like a composer who writes down the notes of a piece of music, you chart the natural progression of your actions.

This is where an actor has some freedom to exhibit his or her own unique take on a role, getting better and better with experience. In drama school, I learned how to look at "beats" through analysis of Anton Chekhov's play, *The Seagull*. Chekhov is a good choice because of the rich subtext; scholars, actors, and directors have debated through the years the actual intent of the writer. In our class we looked at the line, "Mother, change my bandage," as the beginning of a "beat." We explored the many, many ways of saying these words attributable to the complex relationship between this particular mother and son.

Here are some "wants" you might choose from: to get Mother's attention/ to get her to talk about Father/ to find out if I was an accident/ to let her know I love her/ to get more time with her later. Ultimately you define for yourself the impulse behind the line, "Mother, change my bandage." Isn't it true that so often in life we say one thing but mean another?

> *Notice that all these "beats" begin with the word "to" which implies action, which, let us never forget, is the very core of acting.*

Boring, flat performances have no inner action. The actor who puts you to sleep has not done enough work on "beats." And that's the actor's job, not the director's. Many actors get away with not doing this work because it's instinctive to a degree, but there's always an area that needs this special attention. Warning: If the writing is awkward, you may have to create your character "beats" out of thin air.

Here's the vital thing about "beats." They have to be what I call "hot." It's only "hot" if it applies to the character's intent, AND *it also peaks your own interest*. This is a personal thing, best unshared. It is tricky to explain because it's subjective. Can you see that it might be more interesting to play "I want to gain her confidence," versus "I want to make her like me?" The latter is more vague; the first offers lots of possibilities and is therefore "hot."

Many objectives incorporate the following universal desires: to get information/ to create ease or comfort/ to fulfill ambition/ to alleviate fear/ to get even/ to find love/ to keep a secret/ to be needed/ to assuage guilt/ to escape death/ to offer, or to get help. And there's always variations on the themes of sex, money, religion, and politics.

Secret. You can build a career by using the information in the previous two paragraphs.

Coinciding with your objective or "beat" is the other big 'O' to which you must give attention. The all-important OBSTACLE. ***Who and what are in your way?*** The road is never smooth or easy. There must be conflict in order to have drama, to create suspense, add depth, to keep you and the audience involved. This push and pull tension gives you something to play against. If the obstacle isn't inherently clear to you, you'd better invent one.

Time can be an effective obstacle. How often have you seen those red digital clocks counting down the seconds? Is someone asleep in the next room you absolutely must not waken? Are you inherently clumsy? Is the space too small? Are you freezing cold? Sleepy?

By the way, you can and often do change objectives or obstacles. Sometimes they dry up and no longer propel you forward. Sometimes in rehearsal things take a different direction, and your "beat" is no longer appropriate, or you think of something better. And sometimes, it just doesn't work. None of this attention, however, is wasted. That "beat" may be just the thing you're looking for in a future role. And all this activity of determining the character's desires will help you with the memorization.

Ah yes, we must get on with the nitty-gritty of learning the lines.

There are the few, lucky, gifted ones who have a photographic memory and can read a script and know it. Some people can actually visualize the words on the page after one or two readings. This sort of happened to me, but only once. Even though I had done the preparation and had worked out my "beats," I was struggling to learn the blind woman, Susy, in *Wait Until Dark*—it was becoming embarrassing. It was evident that I was holding things up. I'd go home and work, and the next day I'd draw a blank and would have to grab my book. (It was, of course, impossible to develop the blind aspect of the character while constantly looking at the script.) But on my day off, a kind of cocoon settled around me, and I was able to read through the script in an intensely focused way, and it was all there from then on. A miracle.

For most of us, this business of memorization is always different. Some actors look at the words and say them over and over and over again. Some write down their cues and then write their lines over and over and over again, forcing a concentration. Many actors record them and listen, in the car, in the kitchen, falling asleep. They record the whole scene, just their words, just the cues. Three different tapes. Sometimes it's painfully slow, sometimes it goes better, and sometimes, you find the words are there from the repetition of rehearsal or from remembering your blocking—where you are on stage or what you're doing. It's rarely smooth sailing and often can require different techniques.

Here is what I suggest:

> **First.** Do not sit. You must move; walk around. Learn it on your feet and say the words out loud, instead of thinking them.
>
> **Second.** In your mind, you create an appropriate image for each "beat" or section of words. I'm talking

about a picture you can visualize, with movement, in your mind's eye (e.g., putting money in a wallet, pouring a drink, answering a phone, putting on a coat, opening a door).

Third. Don't concern yourself with the way you say the words, just contact the picture in your mind and say the words, by rote. Learn in small increments, picture by picture. Eventually when you visualize the picture, the words that go with it will be there. For some reason, we are able to retain the order in which the images come to mind, but, if not, you can always list the correct order.

Fourth. At some point ask someone with patience to cue you.

Fifth. As you realize you are grasping your lines (little sections at a time) you say them faster and eventually as fast as you are able. Put the book down; do not hold it as a crutch.

You want to stumble, to find out the weak spots where you need to do more concentrated work. You must, of course, learn your cues, too. Some people in the course of time learn all the lines in the scene. But a word of caution . . . be careful you don't mouthe the other actors lines onstage.

Then comes the magic. With proper preparation and rehearsal, you mentally *let it all go* . . . and the memory stays alive in the muscles and bones and tissue of your being. Then you can perform the scene the same way a fine pianist plays a concerto, in the moment, "beat by beat."

THE FOURTH WALL

What is it? It's *the term used to indicate where the audience [or camera] is*. If we're in a box set on a proscenium stage, there are only three sides. The other wall is open. Where do you look? In most cases, the actor does not look directly at the audience. If the person on stage looks at someone in the audience, we say she is "breaking the fourth wall." Few things are worse for an actor's concentration than to look out and catch someone in the middle of a big yawn or worst of all . . . sleeping.

As an audience member, did you ever sit so close to the stage that the light spilled out onto you, and you had the uncomfortable feeling that everyone could see you, and so you had to participate? Well here's the thing: most audience members like to be a kind of voyeur rather than a participant.

Yes, we've all seen shows that have direct audience interaction, but this requires a somewhat different kind of preparation and personal confidence. I've always preferred the glare of the lights and a well-planned, rehearsed, fourth wall that will give the *illusion* that I'm looking at the audience.

Next you will find two excellent exercises to help build your ability to use the fourth wall. They are also groundwork for making a speech or giving a presentation or singing or doing a monologue.

The Outdoor Exercise

Literally go outside—to a park perhaps, or a bus stop—and pretend you are waiting for someone or something. It's not urgent . . . but you are waiting. Just stand there for at least five or ten minutes. Do not sit.

Notice what you do and where your attention goes. If there are other people around, notice what they do while waiting, while just being. What can you determine about people while they are waiting? How and what do their personal tics and rhythms say about who they are? It doesn't matter if it's accurate or not. Be aware of what impressions you get.

But back to you. You will probably do some fidgeting, scratch, cough, stretch, feel your toes inside your shoes, pace, maybe look to see if your ride is coming, check your watch, your pockets, or purse. You might be lost in thought, reviewing what happened prior to coming outside, or you might be considering your immediate future. These are INWARDLY FOCUSED activities.

Now turn your gaze OUTWARD again. What physical objects do you actually see? A bird, a candy wrapper on the ground, a tree, a car, a hat, a crack in the sidewalk, a swing set, a child, a newspaper?

The next part of this exercise is to go to an inside space and try to recreate the experience of standing outside, repeating the same INWARD and OUTWARD directed attention. Find actual objects in your space, and pretend that picture on the wall is the tree; the clock is the bird; a magazine or book is the candy wrapper, etc.

When you succeed at just standing there, when you can switch your attention back and forth from INNER to OUTER objects comfortably, for longer and longer periods of time, with less and less movement, you have the basis for being comfortable and confident on stage.

But here's what you need to get. It's the substitution of appropriate OUTER OBJECTS, that makes all the difference. Think of the back wall of the auditorium as the fourth side. In this case, you could pretend that a light is the bird or a mirror; an "exit" sign can be a tree or clock; the aisle can be the road. You must really look at something—but not into the eyes of a person in the audience. You may look toward someone, but find something real just over his or her head to focus on.

Secret. Everyone in the audience thinks you are looking at someone else.

The Telephone Call Exercise

This is a wonderful exercise—one you will be able to do well and one I guarantee will benefit you as an actor. It has three steps.

First. Choose a convenient opportunity when you make or receive a phone call. It should be from someone that you know. While you are talking, you will find that your inner thoughts are clearly connected with the subject of your conversation. You probably visualize an image of the person you are talking with and where they are. (This is why the exercise works better with someone you know.)

Next, during the call, pay attention to the objects around you. What do you use? Obviously the phone itself, but what else? A pencil and paper? These will be your actual props. Now determine your fourth wall. What objects do you see? A clock? A television? A sign or car outside a window? You want to choose a few things that direct your eyes up and out.

Step two. After you hang up, review the conversation, your props, and fourth wall objects. Now recreate the phone call *pretending* that the other person is on the line. It doesn't matter if you say exactly the same thing. The idea is to revisit the intent of the phone call—*leaving enough time for the other person to talk*. Don't worry about whether or not it makes any sense to a listener.

Within this reenactment, your attention should alternate between INNER and OUTER objects. For some unknown reason, we can actually create the essence of the person we are talking with, even if they are not really there. And we can redo the gist of the conversation. Isn't that interesting? The other important part of the reinactment, is using props and the fourth wall.

> NOTE: When I refer to *"Inner Objects"* I am referring to internal thought activity—images, feelings, impulses, or essences within your mind's eye. *"Outer Objects"* are real things—props, clothing, actual people, or places one can see or photograph.

The third step of this exercise is to gather your hand props and *go into another room—a different space*. Set your fourth wall in the same way as the Outdoor Exercise, where you look at a thing and pretend it's something else. Recreate the phone call again.

Is your head down or up? Or both? Beginning actors often keep their heads down and talk into the floor, or they look everywhere but out toward the audience. At some point your gaze must come up and go out, connecting with an object in front. Having familiar objects there will make it easier for you . . . more comfortable.

Secret. *Here's what you need to get about the fourth wall.* If you keep looking down, or everywhere but out, while playing a scene, the audience feels a little uncomfortable—like they are not wanted. Once you raise your head and connect with the objects on the fourth wall, you invite viewers in. You include them and they relax.

When you are doing a show, I think it's important to go to your venue before the audience arrives and set your fourth wall. At the very minimum, you need something Right, Left and Center. While you're there, check out the acoustics with part of the Gettysburg address, a line of poetry or something else that you have memorized.

MAKING AN ENTRANCE AND EXIT

Time was, a seasoned performer knew how to get huge applause simply by the way they entered and left the stage. When it's done well, it's memorable.

Beverly Sills was America's queen of opera. She took the world of opera by storm because she was a superb singer and such a marvelous actress. I saw her play Cleopatra once—a daunting role for any actor. She found a way into that role that was mesmerizing to watch. She sang an aria wonderfully, turned and walked offstage, at the last moment glancing back over her shoulder. It was one of the best exits I ever saw. It was thrilling because all the elements of her character were in that look. I'll never forget it. For years I've tried to figure out what else made it so powerful, but how does one put charisma into words?

First impressions are important enough that awards shows, musicals, and rock concerts use an ever expanding variety of smoke, and lights, and fire—with "stars" rising out of the floor, or coming down from the heavens. Steps and levels are often utilized as a way to capture interest. Begin to observe entrances and exits, and see what has an effect on you.

How do you do it well? I do know that in a play, it works to pause for a moment framed in a doorway or a spotlight, then walk forward. Michael Richards as Kramer on *Seinfeld,* made fantastic entrance and exit choices. I also know that an actor needs to have figured out and made real, exactly what their character might have been doing *immediately before* coming onstage—life does not begin with hitting the lights.

Can you imagine, for example, how the following made-up scenarios might change your entrance? A roach or rat just ran in front of you/ you dropped your keys/ you just got a love letter out of the mailbox/ you stubbed your toe/ you think you're being followed.

It's vital to know your character's intention when you enter or exit.

Secret. This may be the place to mention an actor's physical weight or proportion. Film loves actors who are slim, but they disappear on a big stage. It's easier to take stage with a few pounds on you.

■ WHO'S AT THE DOOR

Uta Hagen created a great exercise about answering the door. So many actors hear "ding dong" and automatically walk to the door. In reality when we hear someone at the door, we quickly picture who it might be, based on expectation, time of day, and so forth. Isn't that true?

This has a huge effect on "how" we go to the door. We move differently if we think it's the mail carrier, someone we love, the baby sitter, a neighbor, a bill collector—or if it's a Sunday morning. Then when the door opens, our expectation is either confirmed, or another adjustment sets in. Try it.

■ THE WEATHER ■ TOO MUCH TO DRINK

You can get a big boost by considering the time of day and if it is hot, cold, wet, or dry. How does your character react to these elements?

We've all seen the comedic overdone drunk; the subtle drunk is a little harder. The key to playing drunk is to play the *opposite,* something along the line of "I will show everyone how sober I am—no one will know I am tipsy—my knees are not rubber, they work just fine."

The same holds true if you're playing ill. Where do you feel it? What do you do to make that area feel better or more comfortable?

Number 2.

■ CLASSES

Go to the best school you can.

Secret. Jobs in theatre, the ones that pay you a living wage, are scarce and you get work through the people you know. Therefore, you must put yourself in a place where you can meet the people you want to work with. Don't forget this equation:

Good School + Gifted Students = Work for All.

Even after you graduate, you need to keep taking classes—at least continue with scene study to refine your technique. Finding the best teacher "for you" is the trick. Remember, there are lots of flashy ads and good talkers. Many instructors are willing to take your money and can foster bad habits. Think for a minute what makes a good teacher, and you will realize it may not be a former commercial television star . . . then again, it might. My caution is that *you are not immune* to well-meaning but wrong-for-you instruction and feedback.

It's easy to be fooled, so you need to do some research. I suggest you identify actors or directors whose work you have empathy with and talk with them about who they think is good, or ask who they studied with. Get specifics. What do they teach well? Are they influenced by Adler, Bogart, Hagen, or Meisner? Looking at only what's inexpensive is treading on thin ice. There are always ways to study with the best. But you do have to ask. [If the only game in town is one person, that's a big, slow-down yellow light. How can you make comparisons between teachers? I'd go so far as to say you might have to move.]

What else can you do? You can usually audit a class before signing up. You will be investing much of your time and energy in the class, so see if you are drawn to the teacher's remarks and philosophy, and watch the other students.

On your own, prepare something from Shakespeare. Look for or create a monologue, and keep working on it. It will get richer and richer in meaning. [Let me point out that you can use this same piece as an audition for years.]

Read books, and learn by doing. Community theatre has an important place in the area of experience. Most actors have worked without being paid for any number of beneficial reasons—some do it all their lives.

What I want you to understand above all else in this chapter is how important it is to protect yourself. Haven't you already noticed that many performers latch on to "tricks" that work and resort to them in everything they do? Try not to fall back on shortcuts. I'm referring to affectations, mannerisms, and showing off. If you "get away" with using them too many times, you will have an inflexible habit that is hard to break. An actor, by nature, is very impressionable and open to suggestion.

An insensitive, harsh director or a teacher who gets great satisfaction from hearing himself talk can cause irreparable damage. They are not God, but you better believe some of them like to be power brokers. If somebody is "riding you" and you have a contract to fulfill and can't walk away, just do the best you can and remember, *"This, too, shall pass."*

Number 1.

THE ESSENTIALS

I'm only going to write a few words about the following big three, yet they couldn't be more important for very obvious reasons. Each is at least a book unto itself. If one is missing from your training, you will be crippled to some degree. Am I stressing this enough? Proficiency in these three things gives you the *freedom* to act. Here they are:

Voice and Speech

Movement

Confidence

Most students go to a specialized school to get the basics. That's an excellent start. No matter what, you must study and practice and learn the essentials well. There are many ways to do this but find the best you can. If you can't pay for it then beg, barter, find books, talk to other students, work on your own, *watch*. Though you may think you have been born with these abilities, think twice. Even someone we consider a genius has had to learn the nuances of their God-given gift.

For instance, you must develop a full speaking range. A high-pitched voice is difficult to listen to for any length of time. And please know you will not be able to hold anybody's attention if you mumble.

I'd like to put in a good word here for Tai Chi as a way to benefit your body and mind for a lifetime. I think it's a superb discipline for actors.

I would be remiss if I didn't mention warming up before a show. The way you do it is a personal choice that varies depending on the demands of the performance, what shape your body and voice are in, and a person's ability to switch gears.

Every time I see even a portion of a *Cirque du Soleil* performance, I wonder how long they need and what they do to warm up. Obviously one must prepare to dance a ballet or sing an opera, but how about acting? Some actors seem to come to the theatre, apply makeup, put on their costume, and go on stage. Lots of actors do their warm up at home before coming to the venue. Others come to the theatre early and prepare.

Here's what I tend to do. I have a series of vocal exercises I can do, depending on how much time I have available and how well my speech mechanism is working on a given day. Physically, I at least stretch out my body and muscles before the show or in the wings. Once again, I do as much as is needed to get loose. As I usually drive myself to work, I prime my speech muscles on the way with something as simple as saying "red leather, yellow leather" over and over in an exaggerated way.

I like to arrive early—before half-hour. I sign in and then, if possible, go sit or stand quietly on stage. I usually do this for about five minutes to help get me away from the outside world and into performance mode. I look out at the empty seats, check my fourth wall, revisit my character, and go over anything from the last show I might want to adjust. I imagine a friendly audience that I care about, and then I walk around, do my stretches, wiggle my tongue, speak something to the back row, check my props and go to the dressing room.

Finally, here are a few thoughts on confidence. Confidence is the belief in your own abilities. More than a few actors are very shy in everyday life. This is yet another reason a good foundation in technique is so important. This business of acting allows someone the opportunity to practice behavior, try it on so to speak, and then go in front of people and portray it.

There's some truth to the adage, "Fake it 'till you make it," as long as you know that's what you're doing.

Life itself is certainly one of our best teachers. Confidence increases with experience and I dare say, therapy. It is such an incredible luxury to have a trained professional concentrate on you and your life issues. I can't imagine anyone not benefiting from it. Assurance can also be increased through reading, and keeping a journal, and group participation. It's so important to be able to define your core values—a process of evolution. Life and acting are both looking for the answer to the same question, "Who am I?"

■ ■ ■ ■ ■

A DIRECTOR'S VIEW OF ACTING

I have reservations about directors who have never acted. How can they possibly know the process an actor goes through? I direct the way I would like to be directed. And I'm not alone. Clint Eastwood puts it this way, "Everything I do as a director is based on what I would prefer as an actor." And do I hear the names Mike Nichols? Barbra Streisand? Ron Howard?

Then I immediately think of exceptions like Steven Spielberg, Julie Taymor, and George Lucas who I don't think have ever acted, but can attract the most accomplished actors on the planet.

So I will conclude that the best directors are knowledgeable, have splendid organizational minds, vision, good judgment, and exhibit enormous respect for the talent they engage.

Here's a quick reference to what is included in this section.

REJECTION

No one likes to be rejected. It's ironic that people, looking for acceptance of some kind, choose acting as a profession. They so often find themselves dealing with criticism, rejection, lies, favoritism, betrayal, stupidity, greed, disappointment, and frustration. Oh, wait a minute, that's life!

It's not fair. It's not fair. It's not fair. The system of auditioning is barbaric at best, but it's the system we use. If you want to work, chances are you will have to audition at some point. I only know one actor who says she has never auditioned or done a screen test, but she is part of a theatrical family.

The thing to remember is that casting is subjective. Even though you are perfect for the role, the director wants the play to work and has his or her ideas about what will make that happen—a certain look, voice, sensuality or charisma that has to fit with the rest of the cast. If you aren't selected, it doesn't mean there's something "wrong" with you. It means *you may not be the best choice from this particular director's point of view, under the existing circumstances, of which you know nothing.* That's why you hear, "don't take it personally" or "it's their loss."

Oprah Winfrey, very talented, rich and famous, could not get an audition for a supporting role in the movie *Doubt*.

If you ever get the opportunity to sit in on the audition process, it will help you realize how subjective casting is. Just sit there in the back of the room or theatre. You won't believe how quickly your own internal reject or "advance to go" button will be activated. Sometimes before a word is spoken.

Our abilities of perception are amazing. You will also learn from observing what others do well and the mistakes they make.

Because I don't always trust my memory and there are so many people at a casting call, I rate people from 1 - 5 in five categories: Acting, Speech, Comprehension of the Material, Physical Movement, and Charisma. Those with the highest scores get callbacks. And if I am considering you for a major role and haven't worked with you before, I will be checking references on your resumé.

A director likes to work with people they know. Why? Because figuring out the best way to work with an actor consumes a huge amount of thought and attention and, more often than not, time is a factor. Building trust takes time. I have never met an actor whose trust I did not have to win. And that's not unreasonable.

Actors watch each other work. Even when they are offstage with their heads down in a script, they know what's going on. The danger antenna goes up if something isn't working, or an actor is troublesome, or the atmosphere is strained, or unfair, or unprofessional.

The trust factor between an actor and director can be a hard-fought psychological struggle. When I have actors who haven't worked with me before, I know there will be some kind of a test. Consequently, I hope that a situation will present itself early in rehearsal, even if it's momentarily uncomfortable, where I can assert myself in such a way that assures the company they are in good hands.

Getting back to the subject of rejection, let me mention reviews. *They're called critics because they are looking to find fault.* Many actors don't read reviews because they can have an unwanted effect. They are hard to ignore, however, since everyone talks about them, or posts them, or refers to them (especially if they're positive), so you need to prepare yourself. You can always say you want to wait until the show closes before reading them.

THE AUDITION

If you are auditioning for a specific play and can familiarize yourself with the script before being seen, it's a great help. Some actors will memorize something from the script. More often, it's a cold reading.

Frequently you see a cast breakdown [a list of the characters with a brief description]. Then you ask or are asked to read for a certain role. You are given a few pages to look at and are then called in to read it with someone. There are some actors who excel at cold readings and others who hate them. If you hate them because you don't do it well, it's okay. Ask to see the scene in advance, or ask if you can prepare and come back later to read. You have every right to present yourself well.

When reading for a role, you might ask yourself if the assigned scene was chosen for a reason. What little hint can you show them about the character? Is there an appropriate build, a pause, an inflection you can insert? If you can't tell what the character "wants" in the scene, make something up. **It's better to be wrong than dull.**

If you are doing a general audition, and are asked to do a prepared piece, the best advice I can give you is to *do something you have performed*. If you have done it on stage, you have already dealt with nerves and that gives you a leg up. It also makes a difference if you've lived with the material for awhile. Throwing something together in a week and facing strangers may be one of the most stressful things an actor can do.

Often you are asked to have something modern and something classical. That can be translated to mean something current using everyday speech and something more presentational like poetry. If you can work in a beginning, middle, and end—with a build of some sort—that's advantageous. But please, please keep it short. No more than two or three minutes for each. If I need more, I'll give you some direction and ask you to do it again.

As the director, *I'm looking to see if you are believable, focused, comfortable in your body, and can handle language*. If, for example, you chose to do something from Shakespeare, I don't care if it's age appropriate or a man's or woman's speech.

Bring an 8 x 10″ photo and resumé. This is your calling card—the reference a director needs after seeing hundreds of actors. I write my notes on the resumé and I keep most of them for many years.

How do you get the best possible photo? Analyze some you like. What kind of background do you want? Is the camera looking up, down, or straight on? How much make up? Retouching? Head only or from the waist up? How big a smile? Trends change but the good head shots look alive and professional.

Ask around, "Who did your head shot?" One name will eventually emerge as the person you want to do yours. You only need one, maybe two, and they can be used for a while. With or without glasses, mustache, different hairstyle, big smile or little smile doesn't matter.

On your resumé, I want to know the role you played, in what production, and with what company. Example:

Beatrice	MUCH ADO ABOUT NOTHING	Barter Theater

Include where you went to school or with whom you might have studied. If you aren't proud of something you did, don't put it in your resumé. It doesn't matter to me if you have 2 or 102 credits on your resumé—just don't include that phony category, "Representative Roles." [Roles in which you feel you would be excellent.]

I must also have your name, contact numbers, union affiliation, real height, and any schedule conflicts.

I've included the titles of a few helpful books at the end, with more information about the business side of being an actor.

Lastly, make sure you stand up for at least part of the audition. Take time to set your fourth wall before you start because *you must find ways to look up and out* even if you are reading from a script. I prefer you not look right at me, and it's easier on you if you don't, because I may be writing while you are doing your thing—and that can distract you.

THE WORDS

Many actors believe that they can't learn a script until it's blocked. However, the blocking can't ultimately be determined until the actors put down the script and know what "beat" or intention they're playing. All you have to memorize is the scene that's being worked on. A script can become a crutch if you hang on to it too long. When an actor clings to a script for weeks, the rehearsal process often grinds to a halt for a day or two once they finally put it down. If you are shooting a movie, you don't get to carry a script around.

I'd like to mention here that daytime television actors are something to behold. I was on a set one day and was very impressed. It went like this: read-through, blocking, wardrobe, run-through, notes, makeup, and then, show time—live, on camera. I observed one leading actor get no less than 35 technical notes after the run-through, (lean in on this line so the camera can shoot over your shoulder, the light will hit you better if you are near the chair, etc.) and he did *everything* flawlessly. Bravo!

An actor in a movie needs this kind of skill. And I can only guess at the refined imagination, technique, and patience needed to work in front of a green screen.

Let me tell you about observing the rehearsals of my favorite stage director, Anne Bogart, and her skilled SITI Company. This group gives sparkling new definition to theatre as a relevant art form. None of her actors have scripts in their hands during blocking. They arrive at rehearsal having memorized the scene to be staged. It doesn't matter if the words are perfect. They reach perfection with the natural repetition of rehearsal.

From the beginning, Bogart uses appropriate sound to underscore the scene. By concentrating on the character objectives, within the determined circumstance, the stage business little by little unfolds. Through this kinesthetic process, the words, the music, and the intent are integrated. The actors "get it in their bones."

There is a sense of living dangerously inherent in this approach which gives an extra charge to the production.

And while on this topic, I know it is oh so hard, but don't exhibit frustration when you forget your lines. Be aware that others are working, too. Try as hard as you can not to utter a string of expletives. Just hold focus, and call, "Line, please."

COME PREPARED

Someone has said this business of acting is a kind of ordered chaos. I like that image because it captures the courage it takes.

Once again, do the preparation, get the basics down. Then you can be spontaneous and free.

What is this preparation? You must arrive at rehearsal knowing your character, able to answer the questions: Who am I? Where am I? What do I want? What's in my way? What do I do to get what I want?

It is not a director's job to give you this data. You have to bring something to the rehearsal for your performance to be authentic.

Learn the words. Exhibit patience. Cooperate. Take care of yourself. Bring what you need with you. Be professional.

CARRY A PENCIL

A pet peeve of a director is an actor without a pencil. Do not use a pen.

WRITE DOWN YOUR BLOCKING

Another pet peeve is someone who doesn't take the time to record *what* they do and *when* they do it. Chances are, the next time through the scene, they will hold everything up by forgetting the blocking and have to get it from the busy stage manager. [See page 14 for examples of blocking *shorthand*.]

Sometimes you can't write things down in the moment, as you create or work the blocking out, but ask for a minute to write before moving on to the next scene. See the stage manager after rehearsal to clear up any confusion.

After you start running the scene within the context of the whole piece, expect that some of the blocking may be adjusted or completely change.

TIME

There is never enough time. It will feel like the director is pushing you in the first week of rehearsal. It's true. There is so much to do. Do your best to keep up. It will work out.

Speaking of time, be mindful of how long you engage me (the director) in conversation before, during, and after rehearsal, and please confine our talk to the creative process we're engaged in. Much as I care about you, and probably need a new soup recipe, my eyes will float away. Believe me, the other actors notice if someone monopolizes a director's time, and it does not sit well.

DON'T UPSTAGE

Share the scene. Don't upstage or stand downstage of your partner unless directed otherwise. Keep your focus on them when they are talking. Do not fidget. Know where you are in relation to the other actors. Form an interesting stage picture—not a straight line. You may need to adjust your position slightly. Help the other actor by countering when he or she crosses. Try to stay at least three feet apart from the other actors. Shift your weight or body position a little before you speak to help guide the audiences eye.

If you want to know more about upstaging, watch Annette Bening's delicious performance in the movie *Being Julia*.

STAY AWAY FROM THE FURNITURE

It must be an instinct to touch, stand behind, or stand near a piece of furniture or lectern on stage. We can see you better if you don't do that—stay open. You have more stage presence if you are not cut off at the waist by standing behind something.

THE STAGE MANAGER

R. E. S. P. E. C. T. One of the most difficult jobs in the business is the job of stage manager. This position functions as a go-between for the director, producer, talent, and crew. This person runs the rehearsals and is coordinator, peacemaker, scheduler, and problem solver. This position requires a unique ability to straddle the fence between the practical and the artistic. When the director leaves, the stage manager is charged with both running and maintaining the show. On behalf of the director, he or she is authorized to give notes to an actor.

He or she is the proper avenue for all questions, requests, appointments—anything that has any bearing on the play. It's your job to let the stage manager know where you are during rehearsal hours. Tell the stage manager if you are contagious, running out to the car, going to an interview, etc. This is also the person you talk to about a problem with another actor and the person who can get you some one-on-one time with the director.

■ TECHNICAL REHEARSAL: THE LIGHTS ■ COSTUMES ■ PROPS

There's a good reason for stand-ins, but you rarely have one unless you're in a big-budget show. Setting lights for a production can take so long that it becomes physically painful for an actor. You begin to feel like a mannequin. Most stage plays require at least a day of this waiting around, stopping and starting. It's usually okay to chat quietly or run lines, as long as you keep an ear to the stage manager, and don't interfere with setting the cues.

Costume fittings and the dress parade also require patience and respect. *Always* hang up a costume after you take it off.

Getting the right props together for a show is not an easy undertaking. Never play with, fool around with, or take the chance of breaking or damaging an actual prop or piece of furniture. At rehearsal, use a substitute if you can, eventually proceeding to the real thing.

■ DON'T TALK WHEN NOTES ARE GIVEN

One of the trickiest tasks of a director is taking notes. There are often three or more things happening at the same time; all of them need attention. It's a challenge for the director to both keep up with the action, and get it written down at the same time. So listen carefully and be grateful for every note you get.

Secret. Here's the thing, though you might disagree with or not understand the actual note, there is "something" not working around that moment. The director may have it wrong but some adjustment is necessary.

Write down every note you receive, even if you are positive you will remember it. It is annoying to give the same note twice.

Because giving a note clearly and finding the best way to say it is essential to the process, it's rude beyond words to talk while the director is addressing another actor. The only time I lost my temper was with an actor whispering non-stop, and doing yoga, while I was giving notes after a run-through.

When called together for notes, it's best to sit quietly until dismissed. Do not interrupt a director, and do not defend your choice or argue with the director until you have a chance to think it through. Then talk privately.

Because . . .

IT'S NOT JUST ABOUT YOU

Unless you have directed, you have no idea how many things a director is balancing. There are always scheduling and technical problems to solve. Getting *all* the actors, each of whom works in a different way, at a different pace, to a cohesive performance level by opening night requires constant adjustments—along with a more than average understanding of individual process and psychology.

While we are on this point, let me address the challenge of "attention grabbers". . . those that want as much as they can get.

On one of my first jobs, I fell for the pleas of a personable, struggling actor who confided to me that he had certain challenges, and so I gave him extra attention. He came off smelling like a rose to the audience and critics, while other capable actors did not fare so well. I did them a disservice by giving the actor who was floundering so much of my time.

Experience has shown me that "attention grabbers" do eventually rise to the occasion. They are very capable—this is not the first job for most of them. Often, they are used to being the "star," or lack confidence.

My core philosophy as a director is *to make each and every actor look as good, both personally and professionally, as I possibly can.* In the long run the performances, the play, the costumes, the lights, the set, the music, the writer, the producer, and the theatre all look good if the actors look good.

WHAT IS BAD ACTING?

Years ago, a friend and I saw a Broadway show that I simply did not connect with on any level. Though it was developed by a person of some renown, I absolutely couldn't believe this presentation had found its way to the Great White Way. Nothing about it appealed to me, and it was a challenge to sit in the seat until it ended and I could escape. I don't think I've seen anything I've disliked more. At the end, however, the audience rose to their feet shouting "bravo" and clapped their hands with gusto for a long time.

These people were not just being kind. They really, really liked it. That experience taught me there is an audience for everything under the sun. It's all subjective. So if you want to be an actor, I support your right to pursue that desire to the full extent of your ability.

That said, I will suggest that it may be of value to mention what I consider bad acting. It just doesn't work *for me.*

Watching Yourself. Your performance may not be as good as you think it is. How many times have you thought you did a fine job, only to have the director say it was off? Chances are you were checking it out at the same time as you were doing it, and were rather impressed with yourself. If you are too self-aware, or playing to the audience, instead of being involved in the objectives of the material, as rehearsed, it won't quite fly.

Playing to the Audience. We've all witnessed the performer who will jump through any hoop to get approval from an audience. Do not let audience response lead you down the garden path of subservience. It is not a pretty thing when they start to take control. You must lead the audience, ride their reactions, and keep them on your path. Remember that this is your area of expertise. You are the professional, the alpha dog, the professor, the leader . . . not them.

Relying on the Writer. Variety is the spice of life. Some actors say their lines at the same relative pace, with little inflection—it's a kind of trademark. There is no indication of thought before or during speaking. They drone on and on. When an actor uses only the words to convey everything, this is snooze time for an audience. Acting is about what you do, not just about what you say. I can read the book.

Not There. Actors that do not listen will rarely connect with an audience. They do not hear, do not see, do not react, but just seem to barrel through their performance unaware of their surroundings. I know this is usually fear-based, but spare me the discomfort.

Intense Earnestness. It's exhausting to watch a performer who cares so deeply about everything that you can see how hard they are working. I can laugh about it now, but I'll tell you a story on myself that was not funny at the time.

My first major role in drama school was playing Ruth in *Blithe Spirit*. This is a comedy by Noel Coward that I played very seriously. I took the whole lighthearted "ghost in the house" issue as an intense problem that was a looming threat to my very existence. It was not fun and it was frustrating. Those should have been clues. Always know the genre of your material.

Over the Top / Indicating. I refer to it as the *Third Rock From the Sun* school of acting. I find John Lithgow to be one of our finest actors; I waited at the stage door to see him after his brilliant performance in *M Butterfly*.

But I thought the acting style in that popular television show was so overdone, so corny, it was insulting to my intelligence. One form of this blown up, exaggerated kind of acting is called "camp." Although I find it loud, and too fast, and lacking substance, it does appeal to many people.

Reality Show Banter. There is a new kind of untrained performer on mainstream television that is quite uncomfortable for me to watch. Using an ever-morphing fly-by-the-seat-of-your-pants kind of improvisation, they collaborate with the producers in presenting a contest or toxic artifice of conflict. The participants are seduced into thinking they are believable if the ratings are high.

I particularly dislike this "so-called" reality trend, because these shows take jobs away from many committed writers, directors, and actors.

Secret. Untrained actors are easy to spot when they drop the end of their lines. They simply run out of breath. An accomplished actor knows to finish with as much, if not more, vitality than he or she begins with. *Breathe deeply—finish strong.*

ONE MORE THING

It would be a good idea for you, the actor, to try directing at some point—if only a scene. Then you will more fully grasp how what she does with timing, and what he brings into rehearsal, fits into the process. You will observe how one impulse builds into another and makes it better; that ownership of an idea is not important; how disruptive behavior shuts down creativity. You will notice how attitude toward the project gives it wings; how respect and courtesy toward the other actors inspires more of the same.

Directing other actors may be the best way to enrich your understanding of what makes an actor.

Addendum

IF YOU WANT TO DIRECT

I've previously addressed auditions.

Assuming the producer, stage managers, actors, and designers are all on board, and we have a final script—here's what you need to know to get started.

Almost half of your work as a director happens before rehearsal begins.

> NOTE: Unless you are in a director's union, you will probably have to negotiate an upfront advance. Otherwise, you will not be paid anything until you go into rehearsal.

Secret. I find the most informative research comes from knowledge about the playwright. Then I ask, what was the writer's impulse? What does she or he want to say? Do I agree with the point of view? What turns me on about the play? Where are the problems? Where do I want to set it and when? I often search out paintings to get a "feel" for the piece before I work with the designers. We collaborate on a palette (the colors) and discuss a timeline within the confines of the budget.

Secret. No matter how great the sketches or model of the set looks, make sure the designer gives you enough floor space, in several different areas, so the action can move around.

It goes without saying that a director has to inspire others, but so much of directing has to do with organizational skills, psychological understanding, and the ability to anticipate and solve problems.

The most practical advice I can give is to prepare a *reverse calendar*. Start with Opening Night, then Preview, Dress, Tech, and on backward to the first rehearsal. Figure out how and what you must accomplish with each rehearsal to get to where you need to be, by when. Allow time for fixes and difficult scenes. Build in a few hours for meetings and the unpredictable. Allow at least two days for staggering through without scripts. When do you start adding props, costumes, and music? Allow time for notes after each run-through.

Secret. Even though you schedule for costume fittings, dress parade, final props, sound, lights, and taking publicity photos, they each require three times longer than you think.

Go over this schedule before the first rehearsal with your blessed stage manager, who will then communicate with all departments and help keep you on track.

Make sure the stage manager gets a timing of the show, and of each scene, at the initial read through. It gives you a point of reference.

For variety and the most impact, figure out before the rehearsal where on the set you want to play a scene. To block or sketch in business for the whole play, you have to average several pages of script an hour—crowd scenes take more time. [I consider five or more a crowd.]

Secret. Do this initial blocking on your feet. You are more creative standing up than when you are sitting.

It's block and review, adjust, block and review, each time reviewing larger chunks. The less time you have, the more the actors have to have memorized the lines in advance. A musical obviously takes longer and requires more complex scheduling, in order to work with the choreographer and musical director. *One page of the script will eventually play in about a minute.*

Secret. I schedule a private meeting with each principal and featured actor in the first week of rehearsal. They get all my attention for about a half-hour. We talk about the character, the way they like to work, and their personal fears or concerns. I like to determine how a character changes or is different because of this play. I give them my thoughts and they give me theirs. We arrive at a mutual understanding of where we're going with the project.

As a director, I do all the preparation I can, create the best environment possible to rehearse, and then do my best to stay in the moment. I give my full attention to what's wanting to emerge from the actors, from the words. Try something, throw it out, encourage bravery, ask questions, keep what works, build on that, stay curious, sympathize, celebrate.

Secret. When problems arise, pay even closer attention; something wants to be noticed. What seems like an accident can lead to an exciting revelation.

Secret. You will rarely feel you have finished. When you feel like the task is too great, take a five minute break, and then leap in again. Creativity often requires walking a tightrope through chaos.

At least once, have your stage manager run a line-through rehearsal without you.

Nothing compares to how useless a director feels on opening night. If you do your job well, you are no longer needed. Like a good parent, you must gradually give the show over to the actors and stage manager.

Your work is rarely recognized—indeed, it may only be noticed by other professionals. All credit will go to the actors—as it should. They are the ones who keep in shape, do the work, make the sacrifices, and have the talent and courage to be up there.

■ ■ ■ ■ ■

This is by no means a complete list, but it is a good list of books:

- Uta Hagen

    A CHALLENGE FOR THE ACTOR

    RESPECT FOR ACTING

    UTA HAGEN'S ACTING CLASS (DVD)

- Larry Moss

    THE INTENT TO LIVE: ACHIEVING YOUR TRUE POTENTIAL AS AN ACTOR

- Constantin Stanislavsky

    AN ACTOR PREPARES

    *BUILDING A CHARACT*ER

- Richard Boleslavsky

    ACTING: THE FIRST SIX LESSONS

- Michael Chekhov

    ON THE TECHNIQUE OF ACTING

- Sanford Meisner

    ON ACTING

- Lee Strasberg

    THE DEVELOPMENT OF THE METHOD

- Stella Adler

    THE ART OF ACTING

- Kristin Linklater

    FREEING THE NATURAL VOICE

- Anne Bogart

  VIEWPOINTS

  A DIRECTOR PREPARES

  AND THEN, YOU ACT: MAKING ART IN AN UNPREDICTABLE WORLD

- William Ball

  A SENSE OF DIRECTION

- Harold Clurman

  ON DIRECTING

- Michael Shurtleff

  AUDITION: EVERYTHING AN ACTOR NEEDS TO KNOW

- Tony Martinez

  AN AGENT TELLS ALL

- Brian O'Neil

  ACTING AS A BUSINESS

There are good interviews in anthologies entitled:

DIRECTORS ON DIRECTING

ACTOR'S ON ACTING

Dorothy Marie Robinson spent the first 21 years of her life in Beaver Falls, Pennsylvania trying to figure out how to pursue a life in the arts. Working as a bank teller, she saved enough money to begin study at the Pittsburgh Playhouse School of Theatre and was then awarded a full scholarship.

For two years, her speech coach was Edith Skinner. Her directing professor was a Yale graduate, and her other instructors were from Carnegie Mellon University. Upon moving to New York City, Dorothy was invited into the advanced acting classes of the renowned Uta Hagen.

Her first professional contract (with David Merrick) came after a friend got her an audition for a national tour of *Gypsy*. She joined the show at the Chicago Opera House, playing Miss Grantsinger and a Hollywood Blonde, sharing the stage with Bernadette Peters.

Dorothy has worked on and off-Broadway and with the resident companies of Barter Theatre, Stage West, Berkshire Playhouse, and Cincinnati Playhouse in the Park.

The good fortune to work so long at Barter (1968-1992), thanks to Robert Porterfield and Rex Partington, allowed her to play leading roles in 40 shows. Her favorite was Miss Gilchrist in Brendan Behan's *The Hostage*. Robinson staged at least 20 productions while at Barter Theatre and is proud to have cast and directed Kevin Spacey in one of his first professional jobs.

After a move to Tennessee, she produced and directed The *Cave Dwellers, Top Girls, Black Comedy, Quilters, Open Admissions, The Skin Of Our Teeth*, and *Marvin's Room* for Nashville Public Theatre. Dorothy appeared in *You Can't Take It With You, 'night Mother, The Sound of Music,* and *To Kill A Mockingbird* with Tennessee Repertory Theatre.

More recently, Dorothy was asked to stage a production of *Steel Magnolias* for the Dixie Theatre in Apalachicola, Florida, and also to play the role of Ouiser. She has returned there to direct *Driving Miss Daisy*, act in *Queen of Bingo*, and direct *A Nice Family Gathering*.

At Columbia University, she participated in a master-director symposium with Lee Breuer, Liviu Ciulei, Adrian Hall, James Lapine and Jerry Zaks. At the Actors Theatre of Louisville she was privileged to observe the entire rehearsal process of *Picnic*, by William Inge, as directed by the innovative Anne Bogart.

For 22 years, she has been a teaching artist in an aesthetic education program modeled after the one at Lincoln Center. Dorothy also spent eight years as Artistic Director of LifeWork Productions, taking plays that incite discussion on timely social issues to some 100,000 students.

After completing The Hollywood Film Institute training and a screenplay-writing class, Robinson ventured into independent movie making—producing, co-writing, and directing the feature film, *Alternate Routes*.

Dorothy is a member of both Actors Equity Association and the Society of Stage Directors and Choreographers. Her biography is included in *Who's Who in America* and *Who's Who in American Women*.

www.AlternateRoutesMovie.com

THANK YOU

I am deeply grateful for the encouragement, time, contributions, and the gentle promptings given to me by Jay Silverman, Lynne Bachleda, Mary Shelley Carroll, Mary Faulkner, Lattie Brown, and Mary Hurt.

And how can I ever thank my friend Jan Bell, who spurred me onward, conquered the technology, and patiently formatted everything for publication.

— DMR

ABOUT THE COVER

These are photographs of one of my sculptures taken from different perspectives. The back cover is an overall flat view. The front cover differs, in that it shows dimension.

There are many ways to look at the same thing.

The same role, played by a different actor, is a whole new experience.

Cover: Red Stage by D.M. Robinson
17″ x 22″ Wood Landscape

LaVergne, TN USA
25 April 2010
180478LV00004B/1/P
9 780615 351759